I0172485

REAL POETRY| RAW PASSION
OPEN HEART SURGERY

DYONTENIECE P. RICE

HOUSTON, TX
DYONTENIECE RICE PUBLICATIONS

Real Poetry | Raw Passion
Open Heart Surgery

Copyright 2014 Dyonteniece P. Rice
Bookcover Design: TamikaInk | www.tamikaink.com

ISBN: 978-0-692-35178-9

All rights reserved. No part of this book may be used
or reproduced in any manner whatsoever without
prior written permission of the author/publisher,
except in the case of brief quotations embodied in
reviews.

To the silent voice within craving to be heard...
To the vulnerable soul seeking refuge...
To the weak at heart needing strength...
This is for you.

TABLE OF CONTENTS

Part Three | A New Life Perspective

Introduction

Open-Heart Surgery, is a collection of tears I've cried and sleepless nights I've endured. It's about finding a new self-perspective and life-perspective, that wasn't distorted by my past or from life events. When the heart is vulnerable, it's easy to be introverted or nervous when wanting to express ones thoughts or feelings. There were stages in my life where it was difficult for me to verbalize my emotions. Having the courage to express my feelings, made me a target to be judged—so I secretly wrote my thoughts down. Before long, my heart became filled with the frustrations of a girl turned woman whose voice was unheard and misunderstood. I didn't know how to give love, receive love or trust others because there was no room in my heart to do so. I needed to have an open-heart surgery to replace the blockage of a troubled past with the promises of a new day. I wanted to be liberated, *and* excited about life.

Part One | The Diagnosis

"There is no greater agony than bearing an untold story inside you." Maya Angelou

Letter to God

I need *Thee* right now
To manifest *Your* love upon me!
Your love is so marvelous
That I can't comprehend its depths
Because there's so much of *Your* love
That I desperately need to know.
Lord I want *You* to find me
Hiding in *Your* love.
Oh God, I call out to *You!!!*
For only *You* hear me.
I want to touch *Your* heart
With my praise, worship, love and lifestyle.
Lord continue to assure me
And faithfully show me
That *You* always care.

Poetry

What I like to call
Writing what the heart perceives
Is my sanctuary of peace—
My hiding place
From all the vultures of life
Roaming around in search of
Its next victim.
It is here where I have the last say
Where I can scream to the *top of my lungs!*
In just small strokes of ink
Like the glare of a lustful eye
I am more than what you imagine.
Here I don't need your permission.
It is the creed of life
To give of myself and
To be used by God's glory
I
Will not
Accept
Failure!
These words are my strength.
It's what gets your attention
From being narrow-minded
Come and grow with me.
Come learn with me.
Come explore the muscle.
That gives you life and freedom
To do all things.

A Little Girl's Prayer

Dear Lord,

How are you doing today? I ask you to be with
me every step of the way.
Please keep an eye on my Grandpa while he's up
there
And guide him with Your tender care.
Lord, can you send him to me please?
I'll even pray every day on my knees.
I'll never forget the hugs he gave that calmed my
fears,
But my Grandpa is gone now, so who will wipe
away my tears?
His warm hands that held mine so close
He was a father to me and I loved him the most.
Even though I won't see him at a new days start
He'll always be with me here in my heart.
My mom is calling me so I'll now have to go
But tell my Grandpa that I'll always love him so.

DYONTENIECE P. RICE

A Foster Child's Wish

Just thinking about you
Is all I seem to do
Honestly I can't say why
Because if you knew, I might cry.

It's hard to admit how I feel
As I wonder if this is truly real.
My heart inside I forbid you to see
Besides, what's the use, you may not love me.

Confused? No. Scared? Yes.
You are my new parent, will you do your best?
Promise to care and love me
And I'll be very good and love you completely.

One Day

Sometimes I wish that I could run away.
Leave all my problems aside and have no more to say.
No one truly knows the pain I've seen
My eyes flood with tears like an endless stream.

What can I do to pass all of this time?
How can I love someone who isn't truly mine?
Who can take away this hurt I have inside
I can't eat, or think, or even close my eyes.

I'm searching for a place where I can escape
My heart's been bruised so much
It doesn't have its shape.
What else can I do? What don't I see?
Hopefully one day, I'll be free.

I Beckon of You Your Time

I beckon of you your time
Not to be modest with me
When it comes to your love,
As if I need to keep
A veil between us
Separating my beauty
From your touch.
I am young at heart
Yet wise in spirit.
I can handle the
Responsibilities of life
With maturity,
For my picture is the
Flower "Forget Me Not"
In that, I hope you can
…*Remember.*

Knowing yet Uncertain

To know what you want
And to be unsure, of how to obtain it
Is challenging in itself;
For there are many ways
To receive.

DYONTENIECE P. RICE

Diamonds

My words are like diamonds
Natural and pure,
Solid and enduring
And preciously hidden
A treasured possession
Often symbolized with
Love and affection;
Listen to me and hear me
Don't take my worth for granted.

I Feel Something

I feel something
When I look in the eyes of beauty
As I hear her voice dance like
The keys on a baby piano,
She sings to me by her
Walk of confidence.
Writing me the story of her life
Anxiously reading the script in full view,
Delightful is what I call it.
And
That's
What's
Missing.
She sings to the writer inside
Hoping I'd publish her story
With me as the ending to a wonderful day,
All I
Desire
Is what's missing.
I've had a taste of what forever could be.
Don't leave me craving for crumbs
When I can feast at the table of love,
Breaking bread with the one
Who adds richness to my life.

Where I Find Peace

With skies filled with
Vibrant pigments of
Amethyst, sapphire and topaz,
I chase after love
Like the pot of gold
At every rainbow
Hoping love will be
Waiting for me to delight in.
Hoping the intensity of
My passion to reach you,
Will keep you from leaving
And force you to remain
So you can witness your love
Upon me like a ray of sunlight
Crowing my sun-kissed skin
With tender kisses
From your lips
That I never want to cease.
Always wanting to be
Within your arms and
Close to your heart,
I find myself in a 'Gold Rush'
Searching for the prize
I'd like to call reciprocated love.

Crushin'

Comes real fast
At any moment's notice,
With unexpected feelings
That may have an unknown meaning.

Crushin' Part II

Sometimes you just want
To be held close to his heart
And feel every beat of his
Up close and personal.

Sometimes you just want
His hand to hold yours
As a sign of shared interest
And commitment.

Sometimes you want
To see the world with him
Have lots of laughs
Until it hurts.

And sometimes you want to
Be open and honest
Expose all thoughts and feelings
And be together completely.

Pre-Requisites of Friendship

The individual must have a willingness to openly
communicate
And be expressive with their thoughts and emotions
Without fabrications, excuses or embarrassment.
The individual must display honesty, respect and
loyalty.
This person seeks to grow and be open to different
opinions
That they themselves may or may not personally
benefit from.
This individual will learn and practice
Active listening, patience and self-control.
This person must also show initiative, support and
enthusiasm in the relationship.
Jealousy, pride, carelessness and competition
Will not be tolerated.
The candidate should also display self-love
And seek to improve the quality of their personal life
As well as enrich the quality of this relationship.
Phone calls, engagements and vacations are required.
Laughter, spontaneity and goofiness are optional,
But if used,
It will make the individual
Feel like a kid on the playground at recess…
Without a care in the world
Knowing they have a friend.

I Want You To Want Me Like

I want you to want me like
Summer rain in a hot dessert—
Keeping you refreshed and
Filling your need of thirst
When your lips are parched.

I want you to want me like
The missing piece to a puzzle
Of a thousand pieces,
For I will make you see the whole picture.

I want you to want me like
A glass of cold milk
With chocolate chip cookies
Fresh out of the oven;
I will satisfy your cravings.

I want you to want me like
Fuel in your car and
Keys in the ignition,
Without me nothing gets started.

I want you to want me like
You have lost something—
That way, your drive to keep me
Close to you will never fade away.

A Distance Look

I see you from a distance
When you're right by my side,
Yet I wish I could see you closer
So I wouldn't have to hide.

Your intellect, style and wisdom
I certainly admire;
But your quest for more knowledge
Burns my heart like fire.

If I told you the truth
And left nothing unsaid,
Would you come a little closer
Or secretly hide away instead?

A Man's Perspective

What is a man's perspective?
On a woman who is confident and secure,
A woman that is excellence in motion
Without any trace of shame or guilt?

Does this kind of woman appear to be
A lost memory in the depths of time?
Never to be found
Even if
Time—stood still?

What is a man's perspective?
On a woman who is strong enough to birth the
world,
Yet walks with elegant grace and mystery
That makes man desire to uphold her safely in his
heart.

Eyes of Love

I could look for love
But I don't know where he lives.
I could leave love a message
But he might not call back.

How long do I have to pretend
Not to look for love,
So that he will one day
Come looking for me?

Tickle Me

Your eyes tickle me with gestures of lust
Seeing my inner desires
Come closer to me and tickle me some more
And my laughs will be your dreams.

Tickle my lips as you lick yours
As you invite me for a taste,
Closer I've moved only to find
You've suddenly picked up the pace.

Tickle me slow—then tickle me fast
Tickle me soft—then tickle me hard
Don't let me escape from you
Leaving a laugh unheard.

Fulfillment

I wish to hope
In the undying love
So many philosophers
Speak of.
To know for certain
I can take love
With me always,
Kind of like the
Fragrance of my hair,
I want to be
Reminded of how
Good love smells,
How good love can be,
How powerful love can be.
Love is sweeter
Than what honey bees look for;
It's the reason my heart
Will always want more
Of that secret spice of life;
I like to call it *fulfillment*.

Nameless Picture

Too handsome to be mine
And not close enough for a word,
I stare at your picture as
Nothing exciting occurred.

I see your blue eyes
Without seeing your heart,
Your caramel complexion is courteous
While your body is a work of art.

To stumble upon your lips
Would be deadly for my sake,
With the slightest touch of your venom
Everything in me would wake.

If I could spend one day
To know you for myself,
There's a good chance I'd see
That you are the one for me.

But that day will never come
Because you rest in a frame,
Yet I wish someone like you
Could know my name.

A Sense of Nature

The wind is strong and powerful
It moves so freely in union and in chaos.

The wind comes and goes as it pleases
Never asking permission to move.

Although the wind's destination is desperately
pursued
It can change direction so unpredictably.

Everyone sees the effects of the wind
In its destruction and in its perfection.

The wind cannot be seen
But its presence can be felt.

Sometimes I wish that I were like the wind...

Skinny Pig

The more I eat
The more I want to discard it.
I'm tired of who I am
'Cause all I am comes and goes.
Compare myself—yes.
Love myself—no.
Thinness would be best
But how far should I go?
Can anyone stop my hunger?
For food I am without
I just want to be thin
"Hey, what are these IV needles about"?

Sinking

So many emotions lie inside my heart
So deep, they vanish
One...
By...
One...
With no account of their presence.
I run to save my emotions from dying
Within me,
Yet it's a steady challenge
Especially, when you're not strong
Enough to save yourself.
My divine nature is being destroyed
Right before my own eyes,
As I helplessly
Watch
And hope
To be rescued.

Part Two | The Procedure

"Yea, though I walk through the valley of the shadow of death, I will fear no evil..." Psalm 23:4 (KJV)

I Give You My Heart

Lord, here I hold my heart
In the very palm of my hands;
Ready to give to *You*
So that *Your* love
Will fill my heart
By overflowing in the likeness
Of *You* each second
That my heart beats.

DYONTENIECE P. RICE

Awakened Before Dawn

Awakened this morning
Tired of chasing dreams
Which did everything
But come true.
Didn't see a reason to keep
Wishful thinking
And counting sheep;
Hoping for
A peaceful night
With sparkling stars
Crowded with imagination
Of make-believe,
Trust me when I say
Words are just words…
That I don't obtain my strength from,
Especially when these same promises
Emerge from lying tongues
And smiling eyes.
I…walk…away—
Without shame or regret,
Not to be concerned
With others deceptive agendas
Or fictitious feelings of distress.
I awakened this morning
And saw the only freedom
I have is now.
And I choose to occupy the area
Between my mind and soul
With substance,
With *the truth* and *the guarantee*
That I must endure
Without your goodnight kiss.

By The Glass Window

At a table I sit
All by myself
While I'm surrounded
By people similar as me
Yet so far off
The road that I'm traveling on.
I analyze each move
That people make
When they come in contact with me
Questioning their motives
Their hidden meanings
Of the little and big
Things they say and do.
So is that why I sit alone
With five empty seats
Available next to me?
Will someone ever come and join me?
I'll still sit here
For I enjoy the quiet time
By this glass window.

Closed Door, Open Heart

Being separated from my past
I find myself wearing a mask
So no one will truly see
The color that lies in me.
Nobody wants to know this girl behind the fake smile
Or even her number to dial.
Behind closed doors is where I can be real
It's only here that my tears can be revealed.

My Greatest Fear

It's taken me each day
To realize my greatest fear;
The one thing that totally
Terrifies me beyond recognition.
My greatest fear is this:
To stand before God
And not totally completed
Everything *He* has asked of me.
To have fallen short
From where *He* intended me to be.
To have wondered off the path
That *He* set before me.
To have displeased my Father
And brought disgrace to *His* name
By the lifestyle that I chose to live.
This is my greatest fear.

Right Now

Right now…I need you.
Overwhelmed with the sadness
Of your absence,
Confused by the silence of your call
Holding back the mid-day dew in my eyes
From running down my face
I need you.
Rush to my side
Like the swirling of uniformed winds
Traveling across the Oklahoma plain,
Mighty, unstoppable, and prevailing
I need you!
The fruit of my pain is bitter
Unable to alter my façade,
Unable to shield my own truths
My days with you were peaceful,
As our moments were filled with
Melodies of songbirds
And whispers from the ocean shore—
I could rest under your shadow.
Right now, not tomorrow *but—*
Right
Now
Right Now!
I need you!
I need you.

Impostor of Affection

Something I thought was true
A feeling I had for you,
I thought this was real
But it only came to steal.

It seemed to last forever
How it came wasn't clever,
On my own will I accepted
What later I only regretted.

From now on, my guard will stay up
Because I refuse again to be struck,
I'm stronger now than before
And it's harder now, to get through my door.

Winters Morning

Looking into your eyes
I see no life behind them
Even though I feel your
Heart beating
Mine use to skip a beat
When you called my name
When you smiled and held
My hand close to your heart
The same place where I use to rest
Has changed into my nightmare
And the moments we use to share
Time will not replace,
For there is no life behind the eyes that
Brought me warmth,
All I know and feel is
The coldness of winters morning.

Life Without Love

It's Christmas Eve, the day before my heart will
be broken
So let me drown my sorrows now,
Let me try and ease the pain now
So that tomorrow I won't have to cry as much.

There's nothing more that I want, than to be with
you
Yet when I can't have you to myself
Then what is a woman to do?
Prepare myself for the worst
So that one day I can smile.

Pain and heartache I do not bring on myself
Nor is it something that I want to hold in my
heart;
Yet when love is not attracted to my heart
I have to fill that void somehow.

No one can understand
The lonely and abandoned heart
For to be abandoned is just like dying slowly;
So what can I do to kill myself quickly
To end the pain,
The confusion,
And waste of a life
Without love.

Forsaken

If loving you is as
Food to my bones,
Money in my pocket,
And clothes upon my body,
Then tell me why am I
Starving,
Broke
And naked?
Look at you with your
Strong physique and comforting warmth;
Maybe I was a fool to think
That you my *brotha* would really care.
You're the father I see
On national holidays
The lover that's just not close enough,
And the son who never listens.
Why do I love you so much
That it literally hurts me
To wish that one day you'll notice.

Emotional Roller Coaster

Emotional roller coaster
Is the ride you have me on
Due to your inconsistent ways
Which keeps your promises broken
Before they are made.
I want to believe your sincerity
Even in difficult times;
For sometimes the things you reveal
Are so unrealistic to me
That is makes me guess your every move.
The unexpected turns
And abrupt speed changes
Leaves me afraid
To look and see what lies ahead.
Sometimes I scream from the rush I get
On this ride,
Yet you do not hear me.
You've told me once before
That I could be your wife one day
I don't see what you see
Nor do I feel what you feel.
I'm afraid to get off of this ride
Because this might be my last.
So what do I do?
I have no choice but to sit in my seat
Yet should I settle for second best
Or wait and obtain
The first place prize.

.

Broken Love

Like the shattered pieces of my soul,
I thought our love would never grow cold.
Tears in my heart that never reached my eye,
To live without you, I'll just have to try.
I gaze at your picture still in its frame
Why you left was totally my blame.
Through everything you were there for me
But, I was just too busy to see.
I would try and tell you I wouldn't be busy for
long,
But when I looked up, you had already gone.

All I really wanted was for you to understand,
You got tired of waiting, so you found another
man.
I truly wanted to work things out with you
But if I couldn't, there was nothing else I could
do.
So you moved on with your life without me in it
But deep down you still loved me and couldn't
admit it.
So as my shattered soul begins to mend
I'll always wish the love we had didn't have to
end.

A Father's Crime

He came with regret on his shoulders
Hoping to fulfill lost time;
He confessed his mistakes and ignorance
And long ago he should have resigned.

He said he was troubled of what might take place
But craved for a deep connection,
Yet he had prolonged our meeting
As though he was a fugitive on the run.

This fugitive stole priceless valuables
The ones that could've made me whole
He could have changed this outcome
But instead,—
He raped my soul.

Expecting to forget the past
He wishes that I'd come to;
His words are misleading
Only showing his actions are true.

He disappeared from the deep ocean in my heart
The place where his shattered promises lay,
Only now do I experience his
Betrayal of kisses.

My Letter to Destiny

(Dedicated to my sister Destiny Elizabeth Melton
born on May 25, 2000 with an enlarged heart. She
returned it back to God on November 4, 2003.)

I miss you dearly
Yet I can't speak of your existence
To anyone while you were here on Earth;
And yet I have all the ingredients
To give account to the inspiration
That you gave me,
I have no ears that will listen.
That brief moment that we spent
I didn't know it would be our last.
I didn't get to see you or hear you
Before Destiny came after you;
Was that for my good?
I don't know if it was or not.
All I know is that I miss you,
I really miss you little sister!
Nobody
But
God
Can grasp my selfishness;
Not even my mother
Recognizes my fine-printed writings.

As I play on this playground called Earth—
You're playing in Heaven's paradise
With all the other children who were gone to
soon.
I can even see you smiling
I just hope my love can still reach you
Until I see you again.

The Essence of Destiny

(I recited this poem at my sister Destiny's
"Celebration of Life Ceremony". This poem is
imprinted on her memorial stone.)

Purpose unknown to man
But pre-ordained by God
For the use of His will and perfect plan
The Essence of Destiny.

Beyond human power or control
A masterpiece in motion
Orchestrated by the Master Himself
The Essence of Destiny.

An opportunity for all to see
The King and His Kingdom and all His riches
Through the workings of an Angel
The Essence of Destiny.

A special delivery
Radiant and overflowing with abundance
From the heart of God to ours
The Essence of Destiny.

My Letter to Nanny and Pawpaw

I was happier
When you were here
My life was crisp
Like a breath of fresh air.
Your love was the comfort I had
Away from home—
Around strangers
Where I laid my head.
My tears dried like rain
And I still see Nanny's face
The day Honey—dried up.

It was the peace of your company
That got me through my adolescence days
And now in my adult life,
I still long for the safety you gave.
That calming reassurance
That simple statement
"Keep praying, everything is gon—work out".

I carry you both with me
In more ways than one.
Help me find that special place
Called "Heaven on Earth"
Where two individuals
Who invite God into their lives
And their marriage
Can have a passionate never-ending love.

Sorrow Under the Willow Tree
(In memory of Lloyd and Emma N. Tolliver, Pawpaw
& Nanny)

Moving forward to a new year
On the fuel of yesterday's memories,
In hopes of new beginnings,
I think of you in sorrow
And in the loss of you
In the years of your absence.
The distant miles between us
Unable to bridge the gap
Or reconnect,
Hence our genes and optic features
Are undeniable.
I still can't get close to you.
You were God given strength and wisdom,
The sunshine on a summer eves day,
The cool conviction of an honest answer
And the sound of melodic keys in the church
hymnal.
My how time has gone
To never repeat those instances,
Yet time brings about a new day
For me to think of you in sorrow?
Maybe.
But to remember you in gladness and hope,
To connect with you again
In the heavens,
Are just one of the prizes I'll receive
On that *great day*.

Numb

Are things left better unsaid
When one is afraid of change?
Or afraid of the process
That would lead to ultimate happiness?

When love is concerned
Is it better to know the details,
Rather than to be left in the dark
Clueless and uncertain of tomorrow?

Sometimes I wish I was not in situations
That were totally out of my hands;
However, I learn from them
And learn how to change my reality.

I can't hang my head low
Because now is not the tomorrow
Which I hope for;
Yet I won't let my spirit die.

It's hard to live life without love
But it's torture to live life
Loving someone who
Doesn't have room to love back.

So what is there to do?
Words will not always be said,
But that doesn't mean
Emotions are not felt.

4 Walls

Sitting here
Within 4 walls
Of an empty room,
I might as well
Be sitting here,
Enclosed in
The 4 walls of a tomb.

Tired of not moving
And being stationary;
Going about my life—
Different day,
Same routine.
Nothing has changed
But the time.
And time itself
Is telling me
*"Get up and get moving,
go after your dreams"!*

There's a *life*
Outside these
4 walls around me!
Can't let *life* pass me by
Waiting on *you*
To call me.
Might as well
Take up my cross
And get to running,
Cause Lord knows
My blessing is coming!

Like love in the nick of time,
My destiny has just crossed the finish line,
Racing to welcome me
Within victories arms,
I've found that my love
Was waiting for me
Outside these 4 walls.

My Friendly Enemies

I gave them my mind
And they took my car.
I gave them my heart
And they took my jewelry.
I gave them my soul
And they took my clothes.
I gave them my life
And they took that also.

I Cried

Tonight I cried
Because I miss love.
I miss having someone to hold
And share my thoughts with.
Tonight I cried
Because the phone still sleeps;
There's no outside connection to my soul.
Tonight I cried
Because I miss the love
Of knowing endless security.
Tonight I cried out for love
So one day love will cry out for me.

Society Disabled

How long must the
Cries of dying souls
Be silenced by devilish humans and their greed?
Society wake up!
Wake up and hear the cries.
See the tears of the soul.
Don't ignore the anemic heart
Or the unstable mind
Or even the disabled person...
Reach out to the lives of many
And save them, with your comfort.
How long will you keep bruising and abusing
The tenderness of the individual soul.

A Lost Crown

If time is of the essence
Then how long must I wait?
If patience be a virtue
Why is it doing me harm?
Am I ready for my season?
Is this all just make believe
Of false hope of what I hoped
To be real?
Pointing fingers back at me,
Mocking my attempts at growth,
I crouch inwardly
Hoping not to be seen.
The insecurity of a Queen
Who's lost her crown
How do I find thee?
Oh royal nation
Throne of my divine inheritance
When will you recognize me...?

The Jewelry of Love

The rings on my fingers
And the bracelets on my wrist
These are signs of love
Just like one kiss.

The gold around my neck
And the studs hanging from my ears
It's peculiar how all these things
Can bring many unwanted tears.

What comes with the glamour of gold
And the shine of silver?
Happiness that won't grow old
Or hurt that could last forever?

I've been told that love is real.
If this be true, then why does it fade away?
Of all the dreams that I have
I constantly dream of being love's prey.

What's the use of wearing love
If it never reaches the soul?
I found myself very happy
Yet I was never whole.

Shine on Me

If I told you *I loved you*
Would those three little words
Ring a bell between your ears
Reminding you of anxiety
Failure and remorse?
Or would warm
A heart that's grown cold
Without any life without any growth.
Maybe I just want a chance to love you
To just see what happens.
Who wants to be in love alone?
Could you accept me if
I told you I can't get enough of you?
That I crave you like water
I must have you every day,
Like medicine you make me brand new.
I don't want reach out to you
To have your arms push me aside
Like papers on a
Cluttered office desk
All in the way
But never in the way of your heart
To hold and care for.
Actions and words go hand in hand
Like joy in a smile
I wonder when
You'll shine on me.

Man's Letter to Woman

Woman don't hide your love from me
For I know you have it.
I just want to show you
That I'll be your strength,
Your comfort and your smile.
Don't look to the past
To determine your future,
For your future isn't in the past.
I know you want to love me
The way that I love you;
Yet you are scared
To take my hand.
What can I do
For you to trust me—
For you to freely love me
Without any limitations
As to how much
Your heart can love?

This Work Unfinished

I look to you as my Savior
For my dreams have become the artists
On my souls canvas,
Ready to receive a stroke
That will stain a piece
Of your excitement into me.
I want this pale and desolate
Mind of mine
To keep the images
These eyes see.
For it is my right
To want what I've never known.
Seeing in gray for too long
Has made me color blind
To the shades & hues of love.
I can rest assured
For you have saved me
From my violent thoughts,
Just tell me you won't leave
This work unfinished.

Fabric

Cautiously…
I walk…
The tight rope….
Anxious, and eagerly wishing,
To keep my mind focused
On the next step, I make.
One false move
I might lose my balance,
Becoming isolated with fear
That my whole world trembles
At the sight below me.
Falling into the pit of
Yesterday's sinful pleasures,
I can't go back
To the girl I used to be.

Why must I travel
Without a friend?
Since I took my first breath
All I wanted was for my
Father to show me
He loved me,
So that my insecurities would
Vanish into thin air
Like steam from a tea pot.
It's cold walking alone
Unable to decipher between good and evil.
I call love my balancing act
Wishing he would come and
Stop my world from spinning—
With needle to thread
This seamstress is running out
Of fabric.

Commitment that Loves Integrity

You let words slip from your mouth
And out of your heart so carelessly
Like a bar of soap
Jumping between two wet hands.
Why bother at all forming sentences
To express your wishes
If it's all going to evaporate
Like the dew on the hills of summers morning.
I'm far more worthy of receiving true
commitment
Even if you're incapable of displaying it.

Ignorant

Don't disapprove of that
Which you don't understand;
For to close your mind
From being receptive of newness
Is like cutting off oxygen
From your lungs.
So do not cast me aside
Because you may not agree
With the ways I express
My anger, happiness and other emotions.
For to underestimate the
Full capacity of my expression
Is to deny my soul
Deny my heart;
By doing so, you suffocate
The very life from me
That you very well
Need to hear and see.

Another Season

Just another reason
For just another day
Without the mistletoe
To spark unity of a kiss.
How could I get you to stay?
Seasons change but colors don't
And neither did your ebony hair
In the fingers of the wind
That night we danced
Underneath the stars.
Radiating in an indigo sky
The moon gave light to your emerald dress;
Even the fish of the sea
Came for a peak—
Your beauty...
Is noticeable... from a distance
How would I know
That was the last moment
I'd love you...?
For you were taken from me
Like darkness scattering from light.
I loved you dearly and tenderly
For my shoulder was your trust.
These aren't just mere writings
Of a troubled man
But that of a hollow soul.
You filled me up
With your confidence and spontaneity
Now you have taken back
That which you gave me!
Tonight.... I declare....
The death of my soul.

Everlasting Love

I loved you so much
I willingly died
So that through me
You might obtain eternal life.

I loved you so much
That I came from heaven
So that you could know
My love...

Dwelling in love
I came for a love
That my love would dwell in you...

When you accept Me,
You accept My love
And My love will always be with you...

Just as I have loved you
Show forth My love to others;
When you do this,
Know that I am working in you...
I'll love you always...
..........--Jesus

I Watched the Sunrise This Morning

I watched the sunrise this morning.
The birthing of violets, sapphires and orange hues
Suspended between cotton clouds in the sky
Changed within minutes.
It amazed me
For the sun literally rose
Within seconds
Creating clear blue skies,
The only light coming from the sun
I am reminded that my
Abba Father is with me.
Watching me like the sun
I feel his presence
Even when it rains
The fragrance of the rain
Comforts me
As I am cleansed.

I Check for You

I check for you
Call to you,
Reach out to you,
And the common denominator
Is stress.
Empty handed and
Alone in silence
I can't even feel the wind blowing.
Why must I strive for perfection
In all I do?
Just to get recognition or
Some kind of notice—
Noticeably unnoticed
With each effort and step I take
You get farther and farther away;
What's sad is that
I see you each day,
And the distance between us
Isn't physical.

I Don't Want

I don't want
To exchange my body
For love.
Love is a rare thing
The root of creation
But do I have to open my legs
To keep you?
Can love be strong enough
To conquer lustfulness
When you get that feeling
Like you're ready
To collide,
Deep inside where honey flows
From the drought-filled land
Where waterfalls spill forth
From hidden crevices.
Trust me when I say
That I'm curious of your way with me.
But I need you to show me
That love is more than constant pleasure
And make me believe
I'm worth the wait.

Obstacles of Joy

Whom do I live for?
Society questions me every day.
They even interrogate me and sometimes
I even confess to crimes I didn't commit.
Their joy comes from seeing my anguish.
The only time the world is sad
Is when I find happiness.
They do their best to make sure
A smile is never on my face.
If I do smile, it quickly disappears
While they threaten and scheme.
I'm a prisoner in my own home
And in my own mind.
People are the guardians who
Starve me from the necessities of life.
One day I will escape.
And when I do,
They can't contain my emotions
Or hold me back any longer.
Then I will be loosed to love,
Free to run
And happy to smile again.

Please Forgive Me

I ask of you to
Please forgive me.
I've said some things
That caused you pain
My actions weren't always
Pure and honest.
There were times when I
Was deceptive
And didn't show you
Kindness.
Intentional or not
I *wasn't* the best mother,
I *wasn't* the best sister
I *wasn't* the best daughter
I *wasn't* the best wife
For my behavior did not always
Soothe you.
Regardless of the interaction we had—
"Please forgive me."

Oh God my Creator,
Most assuredly
*You have not
Forsaken me!*
I ask of You to forgive me.
For my heart became toxic
And hardened with the sin of unforgiveness.
My stubbornness to forgive
Was blinding me from seeing,
And my senses couldn't even
Recognize your presence or absence
From my life.

What I did know, was that
I wasn't as close to you
As I longed to be.
Create in me a clean heart
And renew a right spirit within me—
"Please forgive me."

I ask myself for forgiveness
For denying myself patience
And for the self-abuse I
Inflicted from my own will,
For trying to achieve perfection
Knowing it was unobtainable.
For every moment
I subconsciously practiced fear
Insecurity and envy.
For every second
I gave my emotions
Wings to fly
Wherever they pleased,
Without enforcing air traffic control
To keep my soul
From crashing.
For every moment
I didn't...love...my...*self*
So that I can now
Live free,
I ask myself to
"Please forgive me."

Part Three | A New Life Perspective

"With the new day comes new strength and new thoughts" *Eleanor Roosevelt.*

For God Is With Me

Scared of the unknown
I run to explore new locations
And I find that I'm not alone
For God is with me.

I see the adjustments to make
To being in an unfamiliar world
So many choices and decisions to make
Yet God is with me.

Everything I need, I strive to obtain
Yet obstacles slow me down
I've even stumbled and fallen
But I fell and stumbled into the hands of God.

Closer than close
I can't escape His presence.
Everywhere I go, He goes
And knowing this I will not fear.

I'll hold my head up
Square my shoulders back
For the Lord is with me
And He will provide.

Break of Day

Darkness has disappeared
Because of the emerging sun;
It is the break of day
Because life has begun.

It's time to give birth
To every dream and desire.
It's time to get up
And walk into your purpose.

Don't ponder the necessities of life
As you sit there in your bed;
If you'll just arise
The light will guide your way.

What can you accomplish in the dark?
So arise, arise I say!
For the start of your destiny
Comes with the break of day.

It's Been You

It's been *You* all along…
The *One* I've been searching for,
The love I've desired
All is with *You*, for *You* are love.

I've searched everywhere
And yet I come back to *You*,
For everything begins and ends
With *You*.

You have so much to offer
Than what I've been searching for,
Let me experience the
Depth, height and breadth of *Your* love.

Cause my spirit to be enticed
To know more about *Your* ways.
How could I have been so blind?
Why didn't I see that it was *You*?

My Lord, it's *You* that my heart needs
And none other than *You*.
Only *You* can restore what's been lost
And bless me continually.

You've made up *Your* mind
To love me, and *You'll* never stop;
The only *One* that I always need.
…All along it's been *You*.

Today's Love

It's your turn to love—
The spark in your eyes,
The warmth in your smile,
That you freely give
To each soul that is thirsting.

It's your turn to love—
The humor in your heart
That brightens the darkest of days
And transforms the miserable moments
Into wonders of internal wealth.

It's your turn to love—
Your distinct style
That sets you a part,
From those near and far
Yet brings you closer and closer
Into the true purpose of your creation.

World Recreated

To say that you understand the problems of the world
And to know all the challenges
One has faced individually and as a whole,
Is to be a part of a culture
And a language of people
Which think outside of the box.
Never underestimating what could lie ahead
Of today's promises and tomorrow's journey;
Trying to be equal
Yet have your own sense of individuality
Shooting for the stars
And all the brightness that comes with it.
To be human and feel complex emotions
With unpromising answers,
Yet to never give up,
But always pressing towards the mark
We as a people, society and nation
Have the power and influence
To change our world.
If we come together and unite for one common cause
We won't have a gruesome battle,
To say you understand the problems of the world
Is expected;
To make a change in the world is even greater
Than giving everyone empathy.

Expectation of Happiness

Expectation of happiness
From unexpected sources
Is what I desire.
Why should my happiness
Come by means of tradition?
I believe happiness can surprise me
From all sides and angles
And any direction.
Why should happiness
Be limited?
Why should I put boundaries
On true bliss
That's beckoning
A taste from my heart—
Fresh,
Distinct,
And long-lasting
Is it's flavor
That it's impression is seen
In my eyes, my smile
Walk, touch and song.

For the Sake of Love

Streets made of gold
Gates made of pearl
Peace flowing in rivers
And priceless eternal riches.
The Father that sits
High and mighty on the throne,
The Holy Spirit moving
Ever so freely.
You left streets of gold
To walk on streets
Made of dust and marsh.
You left the gates of pearl
To temporarily withstand
The gates of hell.
You left Your Father in Heaven
You left the Holy Spirit
Moving so freely.
You left Heaven's majesty
To dwell in an earthly ruin
All for the sake of my love.
You are a jealous God
And my love was so important to *You*
That *You* walked in ruins
So that I could walk on gold.

Profile of a Man
(Dedicated to Pawpaw, Lloyd G. Tolliver)

His heart is peaceful like sunset
And soothing as warm milk.
Strong as a fierce warrior
And sensitive as silk.
Compassionate and caring is he
To what matters most;
He's the backbone in the family
He's the comfort in the soul
He's the child that never grew old.
Like cement
He holds everything together;
With God as his foundation
He's unmovable, unstoppable
Unbreakable and unshakeable
There's nothing God won't or can't
Do for him.
He's like superman
Always there to save the day!
He's a teacher
To guide even the smallest and largest steps
Throughout each and every way.
Like peach cobbler
He's warm, sweet, and rich
Simply irresistible;
And like morning breakfast
Filled with grits, eggs and bacon
He keeps you full and satisfied.
In this lies the profile of a man.

Priceless

The Porsche and Rolls-Royce
Parked in the driveway of my mansion,
The watches I wear
Made of diamonds and gold
The custom designed suits
And luxurious lifestyle I have
Cannot compare to the
Exquisiteness of a
Poised,
Fearless,
And classy lady.
I'll trade my riches
Just to have her all to myself.
My material possessions
Exponential wealth
And substantial assets,
Do not make me a man.
For those things have
No value
No profit
And no significance
If she isn't here
In my life to
Share success with me.
Lady, you are everything I desire!
You are strong,
Rare
…And priceless.

Keep Me Inside of You

See me...
Hear me...
Feel me...
Touch and taste me
Explore me with all
Of your senses.
Indulge in my sensuality
Dive into my secrets
And only show them
With your soul.
Keep my name in your heart
My words on your lips
And my body in your arms
Keep
Me
In
Side
Of
You.

Expressive Language

Words can only say so much
That actions can only express
For on last night you said so much
That I had to give in to your language.

You talked very calmly
Without any hesitation;
Your words flowed on rhythm
And were so sweet to hear.

The more we began to talk
The more I found it harder to resist you;
For everything you said was the truth
That you saw in my eyes.

When can I hear you speak again,
For I am desperate for your words;
Come talk with me again
For I need to hear you speak.

Between You and Me

To my best friend,
The paper upon which
I write, is a canvas of an artist
Used to paint and draw many
Vibrant and poignant images;
The only difference is that
This canvas is the slate
Upon which my mind can
Breathe as it tells its stories
Of deception, lies, and betrayal.
The arrogance and pride of
Being too smart to fall
For love
Which at some point in life
What many seek
With eyes closed,
I am lead by my own intuitions.
Like the melodic keys played by a pianist
I hope your touch produces
The right song within me.
I want to be a composition of your works
With my head held high
Topping the charts together
Winning the "People's Choice Award"For the
Greatest Display
Of love there is
Between a man and a woman
Who pursue God with all diligence;
Yet being One in love and for love
To remodel their lives in unity.
This is the canvas upon
Which I speak intensely

From the depths where love
Abounds richly inside us all,
My pledge of allegiance
Is to the mere scrutiny of love's devices.

Love's Paradise

Goes beyond the horizon
And will never come up short
The finest traits of elation
Reside in this eternal resort.

Relaxation, fun and excitement
And a fresh newness of life each day
The mornings and nights are golden
And the skies are never gray.

The soft winds of peace
And the suns warmth from above
It's here where I am complete
In the place called love.

Woman Thou Art Extraordinaire

Woman thou art extraordinaire!!
Poised with physical and intellectual beauty
Clothed with all spiritual strength, wisdom and
authority
God has truly smiled upon you.

Not just a woman, but also an authentic mother!
Cultivating the vast treasures from thy spiritual
and natural womb
You are a unique gift designed by God
A vessel where His anointing and His kingdom
resides.

Mother you are royalty and far precious than
diamonds
Delicate as a rose yet strong as iron
You captivate God's attention
With grace and dignity.

Woman of worship and mother of melodies song
How essential thou are;
Mother of life, mother of love
Truly you were sent from above.

Today I Dance

Today I dance
To the beat of my heart
As it persuades my body
To move freely;
Freely indeed without
The chains of yesterday's tears
Or the memory of yesterday's sadness.
For the steps of my feet
Leap with joy
For this smile that
Yesterday has given me.

Today I dance
To my hearts gladness
As it captivates my mind
To think optimistically.
Optimistically and confidently knowing
Though my dreams are high as the heavens,
And my desires spread the horizon,
I will keep on dancing
From sunrise to sunset
And each chance I get
For a vision is a second from reality.

Today I dance
To give praise to My God
For His faithfulness
Which endures forever.
Forever is His love
Forever is His promise
That He graciously displays.
He moves in my heart

Like the currents in a river
Causing me to step to the rhythm
As today I dance.

A Kiss To Wait For

I want to kiss someone
Who's fine and tall,
A man so masculine
Yet on my call.

I crave his bulging biceps
So tight and nicely cut,
Solid abs and firm strong hands
And even his cute butt.

His lips are so moist,
Dancing on their own,
To the notes of my music
Singing an enticing tone.

He'll wrap me in complete ecstasy
With his brown eyes and sexy smile;
He's the one worth waiting for
To make my heart run wild.

Constantly I tell myself to
Just relax and be still
But one look from you
Gives me an intense chill.

One day you will come
And never leave my side
Bringing complete fulfillment
To your beautiful bride.

Friday Night

One week ago today
Little did I know
That my life would change
All because of you.
I didn't know my heart
Would be willing to yield
To your every unspoken word.
Your kiss was like magic
And it made my life
Worth living for once again.
Thankyou for your special touch
That birthed my dreams
Into this wonderful reality
As I share that reality
With you in my arms.

Turn Off the Lights

Turn off the lights
So I can truly see you
In the glory of your splendor,
As you give light
To the things that I once
Could not see
And to the desires
I had long ago forgotten.

Turn off the lights
So that you're my primary focus,
Which illuminates my soul
On the quest for truth
Towards all my hidden secrets,
So that I can truly develop
Into my innate purpose and
Remove the eclipse from my future.

Gateway

Your smile is fresh as day
Bright and inspiring,
That when you speak
My soul runs to drink
From your well of wisdom
In hopes of my own freedom
So I can be cleansed,
From all impurities
That would taint
My growth and development
That would try and hinder
Me from partaking
With such sound beauty
From someone who can
Transparently see my heart
Through the cracked door.
It's amazing what a mere smile
Can lead to.

Sunset Suspense

As the sunset takes its place
And all the creatures begin to nest
I lay looking up at the sky
Wondering what might happen next.

I looked deep into the sky
As all my feelings and emotions poured out;
To find a sense of peace and calmness
That's what it's all about.

As the sky grew darker and the stars gave life
You asked for my hand in marriage
And said you'd be honored if I'd
Be your wife.

As shocking as it seemed to me, to you it wasn't
so.
You dreamed of this day, in many ways and as
Suddenly I looked into your eyes,
The truth began to unfold.

As you deeply looked searching into my eyes
For some sense of knowing what lay ahead,
What you found inside me, was not to your
surprise
That we'd be together for the rest of our lives.

Success

The pathway to success has its detours
It has its twists and turns,
There are a few red lights and yellow lights
All on the pathway to success.

There's all kind of road signs
All kinds of shortcuts
And even some "one way" roads
With a few dead ends.

Success doesn't depend
On the detours, twists and turns
The short cuts, dead ends
Or the "one way" signs.

Success is staying on the road
No matter what comes along the way;
Success is persevering and pursuing
The destination before you.

It's an action of determination
It's ambition to get what is desired
And not to buy imitations
But to achieve the real prize for yourself.

When I Think About Love

When I think about love
I see your face.
When I think about intimacy
I feel your soul reaching out to me,
To show me worry free nights
And pleasurable mornings
Waking up next to you
In the comfort of kindness and truth
Of a love with no end,
But abounding in blessings,
I see now that
True love is pure and authentic.
Like a mother carrying her
Unborn child,
There's no denying
Loves never failing ability
To reproduce after its kind.
For love reinstates purpose,
To that which has been misplaced.
It's been said
Out of the heart flows
The springs of life
And I have experienced life made new
Because of you.

I Fell in Love with a King

I fell in love with a King!
Little did I know He'd
Become my all and my everything,
I speak His name in my sleep
I awake praising Him.
Love brand new each day
Always an aspect of Him
Revealed unto me
For unto us a Child is born
But I fell in love with a King

I fell in love with a King
Who saved me from death
Covered my nakedness
And healed my brokenness.
I found comfort and strength in Him
Love like this I have not known,
Love has become my banner
For unto us a Son is given
But I fell in love with a King.

I fell in love with a King
A powerful and faithful God
Who satisfies my soul in drought,
In Him I am never without.
My worship to Him is fragrant
Reaching the heavens above,
His mercies are never-ending
And neither is His love.
In Him there is no flaw
His name is Wonderful Counselor,
A Mighty God,

But I fell in love with a King.

I fell in love with a King
Who wanted me to Himself.
I am never forgotten,
Nor out of His sight,
His thoughts are towards me
In Him I delight.
I live by His words
Everlasting is He
The Prince of Peace
I fell in love with a King.

I am so thankful and appreciative of you for reading my book. If you enjoyed reading my poetry, please take a moment to leave me a review at your favorite retailer.
Thanks!
Dyonteniece P. Rice

About Dyonteniece P. Rice

"I have come to realize that without God I am nothing. My life in this world is meaningless, if I don't have the presence of my Heavenly Father actively working in my life. I submit to God as I submit to my Husband, who is an amazing man I love more and more each day."

There is absolutely no one on Earth like her God!! His faithfulness and love towards her can never be broken; for it is not of His nature to break promises. Author and Poet, Dyonteniece P. Rice, uses her words to capture life's most tender and treasured moments which are oftentimes overlooked and ignored. She writes to free the introverted cries for love, acceptance and thriving relationships. This God-inspired gift of poetry is designed to cleanse, comfort and cheer the soul of each individual. Individuals will come to know that the life that they desire is within reach of their fingertips.

Having faced many trials and heartaches in her life, Dyonteniece is thankful that the Lord has delivered her from them all. God created a way of escape for Dyonteniece and she believes He will create a way of escape for you too. Knowing this, she firmly believes God is using her to proclaim liberty to captives and to satisfy the afflicted souls as mentioned in Luke 4:18 and Isaiah 58:10. Dyonteniece P. Rice is an inspirational speaker with a mission to empower women in being confident and walking in their purpose.

Dyonteniece and her husband reside in the state of Texas with their two pet fish. They both are active members of Word of Restoration International Church in Rosharon, Texas under the leadership of Dr. Charles E. Perry Jr. When she is not writing she loves exercising, making green smoothies, playing with animals and DIY projects.

Connect with Dyonteniece P. Rice

About Me Site:
http://aboutme.dyonrice

Follow me on Instagram:
http://instagram.com/dyonteniece

Friend me on Facebook:
https://www.facebook.com/pages/Author-Dyonteniece-P-Rice/560996767366520

Follow me on Twitter:
https://twitter.com/dyonteniecer

Subscribe to my YouTube channel:
https://www.youtube.com/user/lmalone23

www.ingramcontent.com/pod-product-compliance
Lightning Source LLC
Chambersburg PA
CBHW060358050426
42449CB00009B/1797